THE VISITOR'S BOOK

MARK WARD

THE VISITOR'S BOOK

MARK WARD

First published
August 2014

ISBN 978-1-291-96018-1

Cover : Coleridge Street Blackburn – James Woods and Katie Woods
Author Photograph – Annalie Talent

PENNILESS PRESS PUBLICATIONS
Website : www.pennilesspress.co.uk/books

For Tanya, Kelsey and Callum

No riches can compare with being alive.

Homer

CONTENTS

Hellefield

Rarely seen rain like it!
Torrential: vertical.
Great globules, hurtling past
my window at high velocity:
shattering – dispersing in the road.

In its aftermath, a lull: silence,
the stillness after violence.

The air fills with the noise of water.
Accentuated by the high fells,
it carries the torn leaves with the dust and grime
of the last days of summer, through the culverts
and gullies to the barred jaws of the iron drains.

The meadow opposite is sodden and pale,
except for a small patch – richer, more verdant,
where last year's stillborn lamb
had rotted in the corner of the field.
And I find myself going back – to the
tree-lined road to Hellefield.

The saplings have taken well, along
the ridges and slopes of the high embankments;
the bulldozed bulwarks that once concealed
the foot and mouth depot from the road.

Hellefield: burial ground of the slaughtered Danes.
Appropriated by the ministry for its despatch units.

Blood and bone: bone and ash.
It always comes down to this.

From my window the sky turns pallid,
as a grey drizzle enters the vale: its greyness
permeates the landscape,
and everything of beauty is made dull by it.

We were redirected through a neighbouring town
the night they set his cows on fire.
But they couldn't redirect the smoke.
Iron grey: sweet, nauseous; it drifted far into the evening.
I saw him later that night on the telly:
slumped on the fence like a beaten fighter.
He'd been that way since the final 'pop' of the bolt-gun.

Blood and bone: bone and ash.
It always comes down to this.

The squall returns, gusting, though
with less intensity: pellets of rain
bounce off the window: raindrops falling from
the overflowing gutter, splatter on the sill.

It continued throughout the summer.
Each day the bright red trucks – the carcass bearers,
would leave Hellefield for the farms, the pits, the pyres.
Returning each evening to swill out and disinfect.
The land, un-grazed, turned to wilderness.
The visitors didn't come: the vacancy signs stayed up.
The noose tightened.

The sky outside begins to brighten,
from mercury to silver then pale translucent blue;
delicate, fragile, reassuring.
Sheep resemble cotton grass on the high fells.
Cattle lounge in the low pasture.
Everything is so much clearer now.

There's a disused airfield to the north of here,
where the grass grows rich and verdant.
Beneath its surface, the matted hair and skeletal
remains of half a million sheep and cattle;
in each skull an identical hole, a finger's width.

Blood and bone: bone and ash.

The Beer Trap

For some it was regular
as taking out ashes.
A constitutional. A prayer.

Emptying the beer trap
was a daily occupation
for many on our street.

An inch or so of beer in a bowl,
with a compass rose
of lolly stick ramps
propped against the rim.

We set ours in the pantry.
53°N minus 3°E.

At times I'd lie awake, imagining
a line of roaches
marching blindly to their deaths,
in the malted well of *Dutton's* finest.

White Van

He'd seen some big skies in his time.
Even later, as secretary to the allotment association
he'd managed to get a good eyeful most days.

So it came as a surprise when his health declined,
that he should want to close it out:
a little each day, until only a thin blue margin
in the curtains' folds,
betrayed the existence of a world outside.

He recalled how as a boy he'd been bedridden
with influenza and was given a book about
French explorers in the Mohawk valley.
He said he'd like to get hold of a copy.
He remembered watching his mum baking,
how he'd hook a currant from the bowl of sticky dough
with his forefinger, when she became obscured
by the sheets that hung like sails from the rack above.
He talked of sailing: his time in the R.A.F,

and he spoke of metaphysics:

of falling meteors bringing life to the seas.
How we're all constrained by gravity yet are
made up of energy: that life itself is weightless.
Death, he declared, releases stored energy into
the atmosphere where it amasses over time
to form stars and galaxies.

He talked openly of death – but didn't want to go there.
Towards the end he forced himself to stay awake,
afraid of being caught unawares.

They came for him in an unmarked white van.
We waited in the front room while they
carried him out. We watched him go.
At the brow of the hill where the houses ended
the sky fit snugly about him: a faded garment
he'd been reluctant to leave behind.

El Greco

The meals they couldn't sell usually
ended up on the 'specials' board:
from there – the soup.
The seats were tilted forward
so you didn't linger too long
after your dinner,
and the fruit machine
paid in tokens that could
only be used on the premises.
Yet minor inconveniences aside,
for the price of a cup of tea
there was no better place to hang out.
A meeting place at the end
of the precinct: a forum.
Dates arranged, disputes resolved,
shopping lists ticked off.
People coursed through its aisles,
eddying round prams and trolleys,
crossing junctions in rows of Formica tables.
You could meet a girl; or maybe pick
up a bargain from Fred the Bag
on his round of the pubs and cafes.
It was here I experimented with a purifying
tablet in a vinegar bottle, and was amazed
to see it turn clear as water.

Clear as the memory of how one day
the collective consciousness that
gravitates us towards a particular place,
waived; and I never went back.

Two Fires

Aboriginal farmhands herding cattle
accidentally killed a bullock.

Seeing good fortune in misfortune,
they built a fire and cooked it.

When they were discovered
the overseer seemed sympathetic;

hung identical placards round their necks:
explained it read: *I am hungry: please help*

and sent them into town.
The townsfolk led them away and lynched them.

They were cut down and thrown on a great fire
along with the placards – which read:

I am a thief. Give me justice.

Outcasts

Prolific: profligate,
they emulate the stars in their boldness
and intensity.
Unsung by poets, persecuted by gardeners,
the wrong type of flower
they stand defiant on the lawns and pathways
mid-Spring.
Outcasts, banished to the edgelands of our
towns and cities; flourishing on the sidings
and embankments: empty back-streets,
and the decaying monoliths of our industrial past.
Bouquets for the homeless.
In time the brash flowers transform
into opaque seed-heads: light, delicate
they await the breeze to stir.
Dandelion clocks.
Pluck one; take a breath and blow.
Count the hours – spread the joy.
Come Spring there'll be another starburst on the lawn.

Almanac

Ice

Cold-nosed cows wait.

The water bites.

I tilt and haul the wet disk
over the lip;

ease it down,

roll it to the side,

prop it by the fence:

leave it for the sun.

Economics

Once the head's through,
the rest falls out like jelly.
Twins: bull and heifer.
Statistically infertile.

I clear the airways
and present them to her.

She sniffs and nuzzles:
soft hair bristles as she lifts
the membrane with her tongue.

I wipe my hands on the grass and leave.
Later, they'll be taken away and shot.

First Cut

Refugees, islanders,
marooned:
the tall grass falling
like spent waves about them.

They weren't
expecting this.
Huddled in a rapidly
shrinking archipelago,
their homeland gone

it's a matter of time
before the exodus – of hares,
rabbits and mice, across an
empty field,
as the mower
takes its final run.

Haymaking

Blue sky, yellow field,
grey gatepost, red tractor,
green trailer.
Three laughing children:
six legs dangling.

Grey sky, blue field,
three tractors, green children,
five legs;
red gatepost, red trailer:
yellow scream.

Back end

White gulls stretch
pink worms
like tendons,
in the plough's wake.

It's the back end.
Low sun
burns intensely –
gives little warmth

Do not forget me!
It seems to cry:
spilling its dying embers
on the leaf litter.

Bowling with Sausage Kevin

In order to distinguish ourselves
from the inevitable collectives
of Marks, Pauls and Johns; we gave
each other nicknames, epithets.

I see those friends still – down at the local:
Scratch – formally Steven Itchin, talking
with Sky, the window fitter.
Flour-face the plasterer, Flash, the welder.
Dangerous Dave trying to drop his false teeth
in your pint – for a laugh.

Nuclear Dave sits quietly with a crossword,
his red face glowing by the window.
And there's Gibby, the horse whisperer: gypsy trader,
out on the green with his pint and talking horse;
trampling the crown, where Sausage Kevin
the local butcher, had just completed a round.

Arthur's plate

isn't on display anymore.
One of the casualties of the new lay out
that didn't fit into the story.
It's been archived

I've had *him* in storage for thirty years,
though at times, such as now,
I take him out and let him wander.
Hear his heavy club-foot thumping
the stairs: his stories of soup kitchens
and doss houses, of sleeping rough
and surviving without begging for
the twenty years he'd been on the road
before returning to Douglas, his home
town, and my couch,

where I found him the morning after
a party, among the scattered bottles
and cans.
I'd gate-crashed a few parties myself
so didn't have any issue: made him
a cup of tea and told him if he was ever stuck,
he could stay.
Which he did – for the next three weeks?

I was eighteen
He was an education. I learnt
where to go and what to do when
you're on your uppers: how to stay safe.
He made me believe I could go anywhere
and ride out any misfortune, as he had.
Not to fear the dark of the city
and the company of the poor.

One day he took me to the museum
to show me a plate: a family heirloom
he'd handed in two decades earlier,
prior to boarding the boat.
I don't recall the design
but remember the label:
Kindly donated by A. Weir.
It meant a lot to him.
It was the only thing in his life that was fixed,
the only tangible proof he existed
beyond hostel registries and N.H.S files.
Behind it was the story he never told.

I came back here to find the plate:
the physical object; but it isn't to be.
Boxed up gathering dust,
it is the way of things.
I still see him occasionally,
think of him
with affection, and when
he's around keep the couch free
and the door off the latch so he can
come and go as he pleases.

The Storm of October 2011

When the storm has passed,
copper birch leaves lie like loose
change on the pavement.

Bright offerings that deceive.
Money doesn't grow on trees.

Stamp Collecting

I was never an enthusiast as such.
Couldn't get excited over first day covers.
As an anodyne to rainy days and boredom,
I took up stamp collecting with my brother.
Chiefs, presidents, and fierce braided generals:
girls with garlands; palm trees by the sea.
A world within a 20p assortment
of used stamps from the former colonies.

Jamaica, Honduras, St Helena:
The Christmas Isles; New Zealand, Tanzania.
Exotic names – we'd board our ship in Blackburn,
embark , and moments later we'd be there.

Saw an Empire where the sun never set.
Returned as it descended on the West.

Revelation

It's World of Sport with Dickie Davies
and Big Daddy's about to unmask Kendo Nagasaki;
the mystical Japanese wrestler who doesn't speak
and never reveals his face.

I've waited all afternoon for this,

for years he's been feared and despised,
a malevolent hooded ghoul, taunting
the baying crowd: pouring scorn on his opponents
as he folds and pummels them like plasticine.

I imagined him at his samurai school,
enigmatic, steely, invincible;
his fights with warriors and Ninja; the strange rituals
and customs of his homeland – hara-kiri – kamikaze.

I imagined all these things, but mainly I
wondered what he looked like – I envisaged a fierce
oriental countenance with a scar on the left cheek;
more Genghis Khan than Hirohito.

It's been a long time coming.

The commentator's getting excited and I can barely
contain myself, as Big D forces him down: squeezes
his head in one hand like a grapefruit, reaches under
his chin and peels back the mask to reveal

Pete Thornley from Stoke on Trent.

Body in the Road

Been there long enough for people's curiosity to wane:
long enough to become a piece of roadside furniture,
skirted round with barely an acknowledgement.
He wasn't from there: nobody recognised him,
so folk got on with their business. It was better that way.

Johannesburg in the 80s, a great place for killers.
Colin the doorman carried a kitchen knife in his sock,
told anyone who'd listen he'd 'done' six: belligerent
drunks, who hadn't realised what they were dealing with
till he'd stuck them through the rib cage. Said he liked
to feel a life slipping away. Got a real kick out of it.

He and a friend removed the body; dumped it.
No need for concealment; never an investigation.
An unidentified black male has been fatally stabbed.
No inquest: just photographed, tagged and buried.
His wife in the provinces wouldn't know anything
other than the payments had stopped, and she'd no idea why.

Kalahari Exiles

The car was drinking up the miles,
the landscape featureless beside
a desert road, two thousand miles;
the nearest town three hours drive.
The fuel gauge arched past noon to red,
the raging sun was in descent.
Still a hundred miles to go,
with fuel for twenty at the most.

A letterbox nailed to a stake.
I turned off through an open gate,
cursing my stupid mistake
that put me in this make or break
situation. The track continued for some time,
I began to wonder what I'd find.
No turning back I took a chance,
must take whatever comes to pass.

A farm – I drove up to the house,
shouted, but no one came out.
On edge, I turned and walked about
continuing to watch and shout.
An open doorway caught my eye,
I went to take a look inside.
A shed within the farm complex,
where a leopard pelt was stretched

on a wire above the bench.
A glistening paring knife was there
clagged with rennet, fuzzed with fur.
It felt hostile – *no compassion here.*
A guy with a gun appears
and asks me what I'm doing here.
Tells me this property is his:
asks me what my business is?

This master of all he surveys,
has little time for those who stray
and trespass on his property.
He looked as though he might flay me!
I smiled, and in a reassuring voice
explained that I'd had little choice.
I needed fuel, and wished to pay
for enough to get me on my way.

He seemed uneasy but obliged
with petrol, enough for the drive.
I thanked him; kind of felt relieved,
knew he wanted me to leave.
His manner took me by surprise,
I sensed he had something to hide.
Some time ago I'd read reports
that Lord Lucan was in these parts.

Fugitives from foreign States
can lose themselves on these estates.
Ageing exiles with their crimes,
fear the knock that says it's Time.
I paid him, got into my car.
He watched me as I left the yard.
The sky was indigo and black.
The metalled road welcomed me back.

The Night Sky

It was memorable alright. I'd come home
early to find my girlfriend had done the same.
It didn't take long – It never did…

She surprised me. We were three floors up
with nothing around but air and clouds,
yet still she insisted on closing the curtains.

But why! – I protested, motioning to the window
There's nothing out there but sky!
Therein lay the problem – Miles above

and orbiting every few hours Google Earth's
satellite camera had rendered redundant
any sensations of weightlessness

I might experience beside an empty window.
I tried to explain it wasn't *real time,*
but it was real enough for her.

I closed the curtains as requested.
We'd have to have the night sky instead.
The yellow lamp hung low like a midnight sun.

Light, filtering like stars through loose weave drapes,
and our white arses waxing and waning
through the billowing sheets, like winter moons.

Jackdaws at St Oswald's

are regular attendees at spring weddings.
They don't care much for the ceremony:
the solemn vows and exchange of rings.
Even the garlands of flowers above the porch;
the shimmering silks and delicate lace
of the wedding party, hold little interest.

Encouraged by pealing bells they gather
in the churchyard awaiting the emergence
of the newly weds.

Perched on tombstones; decked out
in grey hoods and widows' weeds.
Avian Eleanor Rigbys;
willing the guests move on then stepping down
to gather the confetti,
before heading off
to adorn their nests with bells,
silver horseshoes and various other bits of tat.

The Chase

Returning later that evening,
I collected the pillow that bore his impression
and made my way up to the spare room.

Rolling my head into the cold crater,
I was overcome by the smell of decay.
Otherworldly, though in the circumstances

not unpleasant: like opening a book
that's stood undisturbed on a shelf for decades.
I closed my eyes and went to find him.

All routes were unfamiliar. Unsure of which
direction he'd taken, I eased myself
over a precipice and let myself fall

through impenetrable darkness; where faces,
some of whom I recognised, appeared out of the
inky blackness and vanished again like holograms.

Formless: a shadow within endless shadow,
I waded on. In time I developed gills; swam through
swamp heaving with the tangled limbs of mangrove.

Emerged into forest that was dense, and thick
with noises – but nothing. I was losing time; blindly
I began retracing my steps through the pathless night,

until a screech of tyres and the cushioned slam
of a car door, opened a portal bringing me back.
I turned the other way. Passed through woodchip

and lath and plaster, the skeletal timbers:
the speckled slate. It was then I caught sight of him.
This time chasing was hopeless; he was light

years away. Unfettered from gravity;
dazzling, bejewelled. Showering sparks on Orion's
Girdle: seeking an orbit encircling a sun.

Trial and Error

After ramming my stick
into a wasps nest,
came the realisation

that while I wasn't
allergic to their stings:
Pete was…

Primates

I *heard* them first – six men
laughing like maniacs when the brake slipped
and the platform slewed on its cable beneath the roof.

I dived for cover as the tools, clamps,
nuts and bolts came down four storeys
like a volley of live rounds on the warehouse floor.

Still they laughed when the floor gave way
and they clung, white-knuckled to the tubular frame;
the toothless brake fizzing down the hot wire.

With the carriage vertical and impact imminent
the hilarity intensified: whoops and shrieks,
loud guffaws.

The pulley snagged: a kink, a frayed strand of steel wire,
a bloody miracle? Two metres to ground and it snapped to a halt.
I helped steady it while they climbed down.

But they didn't see me – didn't see any of us.
Less raucous yet still giddy they huddled together
chattering like monkeys: a few playful cuffs and back-rubbing

before each going his own way. Crunching underfoot
the scattered fallout: finding a quiet place
to breathe, reflect; evolve.

Coleridge Street

Mick was getting nostalgic. 'You'd go down
the afternoon match and get your head kicked in,
then go down town at night and get filled in again.'
Mick Picup, darling of the secondary
picket: doyen of the Blackburn Trades Club.
Dissenter in a hotbed of dissent.
It was here the Beat poet Dave Cunliffe
urinated at the lectern, mid-stanza,
in protest at the local magistrates –
the masons and landowners who'd shut down
his small magazine for obscenities.
He'd published the word *cunt*, so they fucked him.

Mick got me thinking… We lived for the weekend.
Finish work Friday, put on your best gear,
then head down the Brow to the town centre,
where everyone was catered for: gays at
the Merchants, disco queens The Golden Palms:
at the Kings they held collections for
the I.R.A; while just around the corner
on the Barbary Coast punters could get
a knee-trembler by St Peter's steeple
from the street girls. Fighters to the Dun Horse,
pot smokers The Peel, bikers The Vulcan,
where one night I saw Viking Bill swing from
the curtains after winning thirty grand
on The Evening Telegraph's Cross the Ball.
Often we'd end up at seedy Cyril's
Top Hat Club, where hard men, hookers and general
misfits hung out for a late night session.
Its reputation made it exclusive;
in reality it was one of the safest
places to be – people put aside their
differences: everyone needed a drink;
there was usually a truce at the watering hole.

We were always on the look out for girls.
For the most part the success rate wasn't great,
and we'd make our way back through the labyrinth
of terraces to Tim's place on Coleridge Street.
Occasionally we'd detour via
the Khyber Cafe; Blackburn's first curry house,
where our soft pink, delicate mouths were
seared by bhunas, madras and vindaloos
we'd select at random from a spattered menu.
Ring stingers we called them – burns you twice.
Back home we'd put on music and open
our wraps of hash – Lebanese red, Moroccan
black, Afghan gold: the names sounded exotic
and we'd ritually pass joints between us
with a reverential solemnity
that in itself betrayed our ignorance.

Come autumn we'd forage the magic mushrooms,
that rose on wet moorland above the town.
The trip house was on Lancaster Street.
Pale blue walls, a large rainbow adorning
the chimney breast, bean bags, lava lamps and
suspended speakers; we'd drink mushroom tea,
sit back, and settle in for the light show.
We were experimenting, pushing back
boundaries, opening up – we felt enlightened.
Off-season, we'd try acid in the form
of blotters or micro-dots. The effects
were similar, but the comedowns horrendous.
Desolation, emptiness a yearning,
as the trip wore off and we would head
back to Tim's through the iron grey morning.
Lying shivering in an upstairs room,
burnt out, yet wide awake: hurtling
along on a teeth grinding velodrome,
unable to get off – exhausted, sallow,
emaciated; hands seeming to shrivel and crawl;
strychnine screeching through our heads, through peak
and slow decay, we shook, desperate for sleep.

The pains of sleep.

'How was it for you?'
Eight hours later with a cup of tea
in the vacuous wasteland of Tim's kitchen,
we put on a brave face. 'Great, how about yourself?'

Our drug taking was sporadic: experimental.
Our drinking was prolific and established:
part of the culture. Blackburn was known
as the beeriest town in Britain, with a pub,
club or off-licence on nearly every street.
On my sixteenth birthday with my apprenticeship
looming dad took me to The Sportsmans
for a man to man, coming of age drink.
He put two pints on the table. 'Watch me,
it's not about getting drunk.' He lifted
his glass and took a slow, deliberate mouthful.
'Now your turn.' I'd been out drinking
the night before but this was different.
A ritual, which was about acceptance
and respect: from now on I'd be making
my own way. The farewell to adolescence
in the form of two pints of mild was profound.

'It's not the same anymore' Mick continued,
'there isn't the same sense of community
and solidarity we used to have,
where we felt we were all in it together.'
Typical trade union man: we may have
been doing similar things, but we weren't
cohesive: weren't 'all in it together.'
As kids we were territorial,
had our own areas and were always wary
when venturing alone into other parts
of the town: even as young adults we
tended to live within these areas.
It was only the town centre with its
pubs and shops; its hostels, bed-sits and
back-to-back terraces that remained neutral.

Over the next three decades, streets were bulldozed
and levelled, replaced with open greens,
pedestrian walkways, car parks, offices,
leisure centres and new road systems.
It's a brighter town now: greener, more airy.
No longer hemmed in by walls of houses
the intersection wind alters its pitch
as it funnels through and up into the valley
remembering...*the Somewhat that had been*
imaginative lies, like a Cold Snuff
on the Circular Rim of the Candle-
stick, without even a stink of Tallow
to remind you that it was once cloathed
and mitred with Flame.

Choices
From: *The Anchorage Daily News 1992*

When it comes to diet
it's all about choices.
Bears generally prefer the offal.

That's how they found her: disembowelled,
a hole in her gut the size of a water melon.
No other visible marks except a couple
of puncture holes in her throat and
a look of fear; betrayal on her face.

Her husband, having seen the bear approach,
had opted to leave her and run – to get help.

The Bridge

A fishing widow Jenny is,
a widow Jenny be.
She walks the dog, alone, alone:
when he's away at sea,
or by the lake or anywhere
the slippery fish might be.
She meets the girls; or sits at home
and walks the dog, alone, alone:
She walks the dog alone.

James he be a fisherman,
a fisherman he is.
The hours pass in bliss, in bliss:
content he sits and rolls his own;
when he's allowed to fish.
The silver moon within the pool
beguiles: he makes a wish.
Jenny and fish, what bliss, what bliss.
Jenny and fish, what bliss.

There's a place they like to go,
a place they like to dream.
Beneath the bridge on starry nights;
on starry nights by candlelight,
reflecting in the stream.
Sprinkling shards of light that glow
and vanish then unseen.
Ephemeral gold: so bright, so bold.
Ephemeral gold: so bold.

Though they'll travel many a mile,
and many a road they'll know.
The years will pass, so fast, so fast
the present soon becoming past
Where do the years go?
As we age our memory holds
the places where the waters flow.
Still vivid through the years: the years.
Still vivid through the years.

Delphi revisited

bore little resemblance to the mountain
village I'd known ten years earlier.
Sure, the archaeological sites

were there: the temples of Apollo
and Athena; the Castalian Spring
where people attained poetic

inspiration by taking its waters;
along with the main street of
shops, taverns and hostels.

But the large town with garages,
supermarkets, hotels and restaurants
sprawled across the hillside, I don't recall.

It isn't new, hasn't recently been built:
I just didn't notice it last time –
or for the ten years in between,

when all I saw was a pink sky,
an empty street, and an Aussie girl
whose name I don't remember.

Night Shift

Jim Riding hasn't slept for thirty years.
His body trips-out for ten minutes, then
the lights come on and he's away again.
He's seen more sunrises than most.
Keeps an eye on shifting constellations.
Eases himself through quiet days
and the long raucous nights, when inanimate
household objects make themselves heard.

Light bulbs hum like sub-stations.
Spoons ring, before settling at table.
A scratching pen sounds like mice in the loft.
The clock beats time:
                    a pick at a coalface,
hammering hard at the stubborn seam;
thumping, thumping till the light breaks through.

Sundown (*a premonition*)

I've sat down to watch the last
of the sun before it dips behind the hill,
when a long-fuck-off black cloud
glides across like a funeral cortège.
The air turns cold, the light dims
and I'm like, I'm stuck at the junction
ticking over, waiting for it to pass,
unconsciously scanning the faces
in the solemn procession.

Tim, Tanya, Graham, Jules,
Linda and Kelsey, Jimmy Woods;
the whole family, along with
rarely seen relatives, old friends:
people from Blackburn
and Grasmere – all over in fact;
most of whom I recognise.

The sky darkens. I realise who's missing.

P
u
r
s
u
i
t

The
more elusive
she's become, the
more I long for her.
My float bobs on the
mirrored surface; while
my lure – a scrag-end –
dangles seductively,
stroking the reed bed
in the gentle current.
My intentions
while
not
altogether
honourable
are entirely natural.
I yearn   and   wait…

Gaz

His days were numbered in single figures,
it was whispered; as he took his place in the classroom.
His swollen neck made him lopsided.

He proved to be more resilient than we'd realised,
albeit a little fragile when it came to the general rough
and tumble of the playground.

We were seven when he went away for the first time,
returning with the raw pink scars of recent surgery.
I ran away to the fair.

Doctors thought he'd grow out of it - it grew with him:
made his head seem out of proportion to his body.
He went away again…

I holidayed for the first time without my parents:
had a crush, and caught my first fish.
He returned

with new scars overlaying older ones. So it went on.
We admired his quiet determination.
No one took the piss.

That year: the white parallel lines from his turn-ups
showed he'd grown two inches – as had the cyst.
He went away again.

The Cigarette Seller

I was standing by the gate
in the high, white walls,
from which the township clung
and spread, like a scab around a sore.
Inside, the party faithful
drank wine and German beers;
toasting President Kaunda
and his 'glorious' twenty years.
In contrast the general population,
have water and mealie-pap as staple.

Police thought I was a spy.
A 'friend' woke me in haste,
and sent me here by taxi
where I might be safe.
Fortified, protected
behind solid steel gates:
a small hotel and annex
with a conference taking place.
When the soldiers patrol the countryside,
the safest place to be is in the hive.

The guests wore Armani,
Valentino, Gaultier,
interjecting the speeches
and approving every word.
Drunken soldiers were a problem.
I'd survived a mugging by pure chance.
The police harassed and threatened,
yet here the Party faithful danced.
The society itself is not unjust.
The danger comes from those we ought to trust.

She was barely ten years old:
had nothing on her feet,
alone and selling
cigarettes on the dark and empty street.
I got a pack, offered money:
she had no change; ran away.
I followed through the township,
(I felt obliged to pay).
Remaining in the open and the light.
Crouching shadows sometimes breathe and bite.

She ran to her mother
by a communal canteen,
who laughed when I explained
and called the men at the shebeen.
For days I'd felt hunted:
a prey being pursued.
These poor people welcomed
me to stay and drink their booze.
A kindly act, a smile, a friendly face;
can change your whole perception of a place.

It's rare that I look back
at the crocs on the Zambezi,
or the intermittent road blocks,
that made me so uneasy.
The moneychanger I befriended.
The drunken foot patrols.
Mosi O Tunya
rising high above the Falls.
It's the girl who, when at my lowest ebb
restored my faith and gave me hope again.

Tick

It was said of Simon: for every good turn,
he'll do you two bad ones.

We shared a room in Munich.
Scrubbed pots by day,

then at night while I slept he went
through my pockets, helping himself.

Fifty marks here: a hundred marks there.
I thought I was going mad.

Too young – too trusting;
got right under my skin.

Bled me dry then dropped off: disappeared.
Turned up thirty years later

selling lingerie on Bolton market.
I stayed clear in case he attached himself again.

Spartacus

How can the bird that is born for joy,
Sit in a cage and sing.

William Blake

He'd had a hard time.
His cage companions –
the limed finches
captured in the roosting trees,
had no concept
of walls and ceilings:
no idea how to behave
in a confined space.
The din, the commotion,
as they'd periodically
launch themselves
at the steel wire – and him,
who'd been incubated in a box
and knew nothing else.
Bruised and battered;
I was asked to take him in.

I hung his cage from
a beam by the skylight,
where he could see the
tree-tops, the changing
palette of days, silver moons
and distant constellations.
I wedged a cuttlefish
bone between the bars
for calcium, and,
(on the advice of the bird-catcher)
mixed dope seeds in
with his food to encourage
him to sing.
I called him Spartacus:
there is after-all,
something in a name…

I left the door open.
Being free-spirited
myself, I couldn't bear
to lock him up.
He'd been institutionalised:
a lifer, and it'd be
some days before he took
those first tentative
steps – a fledgling
easing out across the bough,
remaining in sight
of the nest.
His rehabilitation was
going to take time.
He lacked lift and flapping
wildly would descend
to the floor or furniture,
landing awkwardly
with his wings splayed.
He persevered

until the chairs, tables,
lampshade and sink,
became as the rocks,
trees and pools of the forest
he'd never known.
He sang his heart out.
I could relate: having
experienced the same
sensation myself, when I left
the cooped confines
of home, beginning
a journey that would
take me to Africa and
the farthest reaches
of the planet.
It's all about self-belief.

The walls of the cricket club
were topped with broken glass.
As kids we'd crush and
grind the shards with
stones making perches
to sit and watch the match.
His preferred spot
was a rail across
the kitchen window,
overlooking the pitch
and park, with its large
Victorian conservatory
where exotic trees
heaved and pressed the
wrought iron trusses
and glass roof,
in search of the sun.
Beside it stood an aviary.

On Sunday mornings
when the air was still,
before pealing church bells
anointed the streets, their
song eased under
the eaves: drifted in through
cracks and vents, stirring
something primal
within him.
He knew their language
and called back in joyous
self-awareness.
The flat was large.
I'd leave the interior
doors open.
He became adept at flying.
Kept me at arms length.
I understood – a room
shrinks with familiarity.
I left him to it.

There's a lot to be said
for a name...
While I doubt he planned
his escape, he didn't
pass up the opportunity
when a friend left
the bathroom window ajar.
I'd been fearful of releasing
him in case he'd come
to harm, but was all for
self-determination:
quietly wished him well,
but left the window open a few
days in case he changed
his mind.
He never did.

I liked to think of him
living among the palms
and acacia in the hothouse:
conducting the Sunday choir.
Maybe settling down
and having a family –
As I did, until our world
became restricted and we
moved apart.
He'd felt safe in his
cage and had I never
opened the door
would've known no better.
With choice comes curiosity
and desire;
but it's never enough.

Beyond each horizon is
another – another after
that and then another,
until we eventually
return to our place
of embarkation: weary,
but in the knowledge
that without
fixed points of reference
we're liable to walk in circles.
My own world has shrunk to this:
a quiet room with books
and an open window.
These days it's the scene of
my greatest journeys.

The Visitor's Book

Five Rivers

'The Sea, the Sea,' we cried! As the bus turned
the corner onto the promenade:
the bay laid out before us – a silver dish:
shimmering, benign; and for a first sighting
strangely familiar – awakening sensors
embedded deep in my subconscious.
Taking me back to a time when I was
forming, alone and blind,
                                              suspended in
a sack of amniotic fluid.
Now it was calling me; inviting me home.

It was the summer of love (mum was blonde
back then) and the vibrant colours
along with the sights, sounds and smells,
made the excitement almost unbearable as
we came to disembark, and make our way
through the throngs of people with our bedding
and suitcases, to our lodgings.

Coming from the industrial heartland
of East Lancashire, where the view was
generally restricted to the row opposite,
then mimicked around each corner;
where the belching factories pointed
rude blackened fingers towards the heavens:
the vast expanse of Morecambe Bay suddenly
made the world so much bigger and brighter.
The shrimp boats bobbing on the gentle swell;
the fizz of receding waves on sand:
Rosie Lee in her velvet crimson
booth with gilded fleur de lis. 'Fortune teller
to the rich and famous' – around her walls,
the autographed photos of music hall stars.
Vendors selling cockles, mussels, winkles
(like black pellets) with a pin – 'careful son':
and shrimps – 'pull off the head, split the underside

with your thumb-nail and peel back the husk:'
the texture and taste, ribbed, fleshy, salty and
succulent.

A balloon; a bucket and spade:
before advancements in moulded plastics
turned the humble sandcastle from upturned
plant-pots to Conwy, a certain ingenuity
was required in castellating ones efforts.

I remember still my first sunburn,
luminous pink and raw; the sand scratching
like glass. Later at the apartment
the baths' luke-warm water scalded my back
and legs; throughout the night the heavy cotton
sheets pricked and scoured, only to be forgotten
the next day, as the excitement of being
there overcame all other discomforts.

Amusements

I made my money that day, on the Penny Falls,
when my carefully slotted penny brought
down the whole row: momentarily fused,
it crashed hard; like a lump of solid bronze.

Half a pound heavier, and feeling rich,
I made my way up to the Marina,
where a rather sad looking dolphin, waved,
chattered and leapt through hoops, for our amusement.

From there, the Reptile House and its star attraction;
two alligators – in touching distance
through the railings. Bored and uninspired,
they lay motionless by the shallow pool,
every inch of their backs covered in coins,
thrown by frustrated punters wanting action.

Sequined alligators – Now that's showbiz!

Why have depth; when you
can usually find what you
want on the surface?

We didn't visit much in the 70s –
except on day-trips. Landladies preferred
the long-term letting of their properties
to the construction workers from Heysham
Power Station: With rooms scarce and at a
premium, we opted for a caravan
near Cockerham on the Lune estuary.
Cheap too – a good stick; a penknife; fishing rod
and an unrestricted freedom to roam.
It was here that I came into my own...

Befriending the farmer, who would take me
out across the sands on his tractor to check
his nets, strung out on stakes across the channel.
Wading tentatively, hoping to step on a flatty –
or mischievously slipping one out from
the folds of the net, claiming I'd caught it!
A seemingly inexhaustible larder:
we'd gather mussels from the beds by the
old lighthouse; tearing them from the tangled
mass of black matted hair that bound them to
the wet rocks.
                    It wouldn't last – The opening
of the power station at Heysham;
the chemical works on the Wyre,
along with raw untreated sewage
released daily from the pumping stations...

Just after this the signs went up:

DO NOT EAT THE SHELLFISH

Tampons, turds and fixing agents.
Harsh industrial detergents.
Nitrates, bleach and scouring soaps;
carried down the rivers, churning round the coast.

Detritus from our modern lives
discharged on the ebbing tides.
Out of sight and out of mind.
Feeds the molluscs, shrimps and flounder,
ends up in our seafood chowder.

Bycatch

This empty gaff was Johnny Whelks,
he used to be a snail.
Now he's been evicted
and his home is up for sale.

Along with skeletal seahorses,
stuck on barometers.
Urchins; starfish
and clamshell thermometers.
Calcified, colourful, conical spheres,
imparting the sound of the wind
and waves,
when pressed up close to your ear.

With the departure of the construction workers,
Morecambe's landladies reopened their doors.
No one came…
                    The advent of the package holiday
to the former Spanish fishing villages
of Majorca and the Costa del Sol
'the sunshine coast', made the prospect of
a potentially rain-lashed fortnight on
a wind-swept promenade unappealing.
Driving through in the late 80s and 90s
the sense of neglect induced melancholy.
All that remained was nostalgia.
The traditional British seaside holiday
had gone into terminal decline
that no ill-conceived theme park could hope
to revive.

Only the sea remained constant
on its elliptical lunar cycle.
Pouring through the Lune Deeps to Lancaster Sound,
over Yeomans Wharf and the Old Grange:
flooding the Leven Sands and the Kent Bank.
Giver of life – and taker – magnanimous always;
absorbing the waters of the five rivers
flowing into the bay from the north,
east and south, then emptying like a drain,
leaving a vast expanse of sand like a
great northern desert. – It never fails.

The past decade has marked the beginnings
of a revival: the sea, cleaner now
than at any point in the last fifty years,
once more yields its bounty. Hope and belief
have replaced melancholy and despair.
The uninterrupted view across the bay
remains magnificent. The Winter Gardens,
where Laurel and Hardy,
Shirley Bassey and Dr Crock and his
Orchestra shocked and delighted audiences,
has put on its first show in 30 years;
while the 'art deco' Midland Hotel,
where the avante garde had enjoyed a more
up-market bonk – has opened its doors again.
The people are returning…

* * *

So long as the sea lives, so shall we.
Shifting with the fluidity of sand:
turning inward, blending through without a trace.
All I came to know and understand.
The cyclical redemptions of water, and of man:
awareness, self-belief, unerring faith.
Were formed within the little boy
who never leaves this place.

The Photograph

Sunrise skims the distant ebbing tide.
Hunched figures at the waterline revealed,
as cockle-gatherers with suction boards,
that pad the spongy sand and tease
the creatures out from underneath.

The man, who stakes his nets by ancient right.
A farmer of the sea, and not the land.
Drives out to haul his catch in from the night.
The pier's exposed backbone rattles
out across the sand.

Deckchairs lashed to railings, shuttered booths.
A solitary gull gives out a cry; and
passing hangs her lyric on a bar,
which holds the note suspended in
an empty hollow sky.

Then stillness, but for occasional gusts;
clattering cables, loose on poles and boats.
Slowly though in unison,
landladies loose their charges, from
their gaily painted fronts.

Now all the town's awake – yet I'm alone.
A memory, on this ghostly promenade.
The youngster in the fading monochrome:
holding a monkey, with his brothers at his side;
on holiday in Morecambe circa 1965.

Glue

Without meaning to
sound trivial. The donkeys –
did they find a home?

Acknowledgements

Bowling with Sausage Kevin, Body in the Road, Two Fires, The Beer Trap and *Stamp Collecting* were published in the Penniless Press magazine *Mistress Quickly's Bed.* Winter 2011.

Stamp Collecting was published in the Wordsworth Trust quarterly, *The Messenger.* 2011.

Outcasts, was commissioned by artist Rebecca Chesney for her exhibition *Dandelions.* 2011.

Bowling with Sausage Kevin, The Beer Trap, Stamp Collecting, Coleridge Street, Revelation, Gaz, Night Shift and *El Greco* were published in a pamphlet: *Coleridge Street* (Aussteiger Publicatons) 2012.

The Lakes Arts Collective commissioned *Jackdaws at St Oswald's* for an exhibition *Holy Detritus.* 2013.

Hellefield, Primates, White Van and *Arthur's Plate* were published in *Mistress Quickly's Bed.* 2014

The Visitor's Book formed part of an exhibition funded by Arts Council England and Lancaster City Council at Morecambe's Winter Gardens. The sequence along with images from the show was published as a pamphlet: *Five Rivers.*

Amusements appeared in *Thunder Alley* (Aussteiger Publications) 2008

The Photograph appeared in *Used Rhymes* (Aussteiger Publications) 2007

#0173 - 230916 - C0 - 229/152/4 - PB - DID1594727